Drifting

Nia Crews

Book Cover Art by Mikea Hugley.

IBSN-13: 9781070841670

A compilation of short poems, thoughts, and feelings

Table of Contents

Mother Nature dwells inside of you
You are a WOMAN
You bring forth life
You bring forth love
You bring forth rage
You bring forth peace
You bring forth pain
Love is the reason you always sustain
At times there's hell inside of you
If not careful, it'll try to distort your view
You are a woman
You will always find your way
You are Life
You are Love

You are a WOMAN

Drench me in water to cleanse residue my past has stained me with

Place a fortune cookie in my hand
To remind me that even after breaking
There's optimism fitting right inside the crevices of my fingers

Study the blueprint of me
Tracing lines that lead back to my heart

Memorize my pulse so you'll know the exact moment my heart beats faster for you

For you....
For you....

Love You

Fighting Feelings

I wanted my stomach to stop allowing butterflies to tickle its
outskirts
I wanted my heart to pace itself for the marathon, not short
distance
I wanted my pupils to stop enlarging at the sight of your face
I wanted time to speed up so that these feelings could subside
I guess I'm finally realizing the meaning of loving someone from
the inside out

Conditional Love

Problem is I loved you on terms and conditions
The part you missed was the fine print at the bottom
I purposely hid so you couldn't see I was broken
You insisted on piecing together what used to be a mirror

By loving you on terms and conditions
I prematurely jumped into an agreement I wasn't ready for
Which caused the lease to be cut short

Problem with conditional love is, it's based off reaction to how a person feeds you affection
So the way I loved you was the way I loved myself...
Self-reflection

Muscle Memory

I wished you called so I could practice ignoring you
Increase my reps of loving me more
Stretch my mind
To realize that not everyone serves a long purpose in my life
Exercising the inner most section of my palm
To release the urge to answer
Teaching my heart that silent beats are still beats
And still pump the same as loud ones
And that veins still flush blood throughout my entire body with or
without you

She speaks to me more often than I'd like
And on most days, I chose to ignore her
Only to realize
Those were moments I needed to hear her most

Intuition

I Wonder

I wonder do you think of me when you travel across the world
Do you see me as a wonder compared to the other seven?
When you count up what you're grateful for do you count me as a blessing?
Or do you count me as a lesson?

I wonder if you've moved on and whose soul you're caressing
Because I saw you as a holy man, not in church every Sunday but you trust his plan
That flame in my heart, you lit up so beautifully
I know pain and love don't mix
But in us somehow, they'd agree

I felt like staying with you I was losing me
But there was no other place I'd choose to be
I wonder If you knew your presence wouldn't be appreciated
Until I pushed you into absence
I wonder if you feel my love harder now hearing me reminisce over our love in past tense

Persistent

He'd part the seas riding the waves of aggression and a tide of tears just to reach me

He'd learn sign language and braille just to show me love has many languages

He'd create a space for peace because he knew I was at war with the world

He'd always have a garden to come back to nurturing seeds of knowledge he planted often

He'd always have my ear...just one
So his words could never escape out the other

He'd always have someone who simply wished they had the chance to thank his mother

Misunderstanding

Your heart was a love letter to me
I unintentionally placed in a shredder
Mistaking it for trash others had previously handed me

My Mother's Love

I knew she loved me immensely but didn't quite teach me how to love myself

She didn't understand the navigation techniques I used in seeking love

But always co-piloted my plane when life's turbulence shook me

Hanging myself with a rope of self-doubt she'd find her way to unhook me

Her eyes speak to me saying....
"Spare me another chance in attempts to save my baby"

Angelic her presence was, I ascended on a hope and a maybe

Running

For years I'd run from truths that would eventually eat me alive
Biting through flesh until all there was, was bone
Bones I felt at times were too weak to stand me up

For years I'd turn on the washing machine
Only to put on the same feelings I've dried
In hopes they'd be something new

For years I'd continue this constant cycle of tossing and tumbling
And yet these clothes still reek
Of regret...
Of mistake after mistake...
Giving my heart and falling...
With high expectations only to be met by a wait

Resentment

My eyes look at you the same, but my heart doesn't
My heart beats the same, but my pain doesn't
Its acute onset has been nothing short of excruciating
Since the response to my question
If you loved her was followed by a
Yes

Drifting

I inhaled flames from the forest fire you created
Ignited from the spark you placed in my heart
Attempting to burn away feelings that still linger
Ashes simmer once the fire settles
From the 2 aggressive hoses placed on both sides of my face
Just above my nose
Can we say one last prayer
Before we jar and sprinkle the ashes over the oceans
Promise me,
When I cry again I won't see them as I float in hopes of reaching
your light house

However long you need

How long do you mourn over a failed relationship?
How long do you weep over the same body of love that has died?
Truth is
You don't put a time on your healing
You don't put an expiration date on your hurting
Each day you just make sense of your **Self -Worth**
And why you are still deserving

One last time

This isn't to win the war of love we've been fighting coming up on a year, but to be felt one last time

Touching parts of your heart no one has….been deep enough to even paddle

Because your veins aren't the easiest to shoot into with doses of love strong enough to weaken the chambers of the organ that's been beaten most

And continues still to beat the most

The Dramatics

Piercing sounds vibrate my ears drums
As I cry out hysterically
Playing back memories with you
Our movie ended scenes ago
But I stay for the credits and anticipate a sequel

The Photos

They say a picture speaks a thousand words
For me they just track minutes, moments, and miles.
Minutes that pass for each day I no longer hear from you
Moments that I will never get back
And memorized miles I'd drive to you

The Acceptance

Staying in denial bought me a sense of comfort
Like a heavy comforter on a hot summer night
I woke up drenched in sweat
From being wrapped up in the lies I fed myself
I started tasting the truth day by day
Which led me closer to the entree of reality

Figures Hidden

What he thought may have been simple multiplication
Turned out to be long division
Unaware he would grow tired of dividing and conquering the
demons of my past

Half full

Half empty

He told you half truths
Leaving you half empty
Because he knew whole ones would drown you

Monthly Forecast

Spring is here and with all the tears I showered you in
How could I not expect for you to blossom?
I'm still de-icing my heart from the previous months
Seasons change
Emotions linger

Gloomy Weather

I remember when you told me "I gotta learn to let stuff go or it'll eat me up."

Sometimes I still feel like I'm
inside the belly of my past...

Similarities

You Leave
Only to come back
Sort of like my father
Only difference is
He came
And left forever...

Indescribable

My entire life I've saw two men cry in front of my face
None of them were *my father*
Mourning the loss of someone that is still alive is a different type of
pain

Empty

You've spent so much time furnishing the houses of others
But have yet to give yourself a house warming of its own

Thoughts in August of 2018

Stop signs for me were merely just roadblocks to you
Wanting you is like wanting water to quench my thirst
I refuse to swallow pills of logic or reasoning
I refuse to digest anything that will wilt the wings of the butterflies
inside of me,
Because of you

Nostalgia

How is it out there?
I'm sure the same as usual
You always mentioned everything you needed was there
But I always hoped you'd make your way to the east coast

Heal

It takes time
Time doesn't take it
Don't rush the process

With tears in your eyes
Breathe.
With weight on your shoulders
Breathe.
With a knot in your throat
Breathe.
With the cracking of your voice
Breathe.
With the trembling of your hands
Breathe.
Take a moment and allow your lungs to work on your behalf...

Breathe

Unavailable Merch

No amount of money can replace your happiness within
And no amount of running could catch that one particular man
It takes a different type of deposit to be secure within

Closet Love

A temporary high and feeling of being wanted
Seeing you roll out of my bed
My mind you taunted
Skeletons add up
My closet
Still haunted

Death by Social Media

Highlight reels and lime light feels
Behind closed doors you don't see their chills
Out of the body experience creating inner body hinderance
Through pictures is their deliverance
To you their life is grand
But a picture only limits it

Worse Day

On my worse day I thought I needed you
On my worst day the right words you knew
My worse day began when I made a God out of you
When we stopped operating as two
And more as one, as if we were wedded
Relationship coffin like
We knew we should have dead it
Resuscitating it when there should have been a eulogy
Neither one of us dared to say goodbye to the words YOU and ME

I made an idol out of this word
I nurtured it as if it were a person
This word to me held so much weight
Eventually revealing to me
Maybe it's not as beautiful as it sounds
And that its meaning is merely a facade

Forever

User Friendly

I've been filling these voids with people
Ignoring the fact, they potentially just look through me like
Peep holes

Don't Go

We all know the outcome when we have sex with no protection
But those phone calls after to reach you no signal, no detection....
Your dick used as a weapon
Lethal with injection
This baby I now hold
Lacks a father's affection
We need you in this world where blue collars prey upon you
Simply because of your skin
We need you in this world to be an example for our young men
We need you to come back and nurture the seed you planted
We need you in this world so little black boys can break the cycle
of being damaged

I wanted it
I chased you down to receive it
Slapped me in the face when I got it
Only to realize life goes on with or without it

Closure

I Know Her

I know a girl who wishes to be lighter simply because she thought
that's what attracted men
I know a girl who was drunk off "likes" she never wanted to feel
sobriety
I know a girl who didn't want to stay in the sun too long because
she feared getting darker
I know a world that defines beauty by the amount of melanin in
your skin
I know a girl terrified her skin would keep her away from a "win"
I know a girl who was told her hair was simply a little different
I know a girl who kept fighting for opportunities "they" tried but
couldn't limit
I know a girl who lost herself
Just to find herself
Then lost herself again
I know a girl who's now a better version of herself
Who knows internal love is better than wealth
And that a love worth dying for was buried within herself

To: Self

From: Love

I see you for who you are, and I stand in awe
To say I'm memorized by you would be an understatement
For so long I've watched you
And to approach you, I debated
Your presence was subtle yet powerful
To me you were a daisy and I like picking flowers so
To water you and watch you grow
I'd ensure you'd overflow
And because the sun kisses you daily
You're nothing short of a constant glow

The fierce
The fearless
The focused
The fascinating
The first real super heroes

The WOMAN

Let God

My hands try to orchestrate only what you can
Neglecting the fact that my mind can take me where my feet can't
Allow me to weaken my hands and strengthen my Faith

A Message To The Most High

Thank you for keeping me
Day after day
Even on days when I found myself not wanting to be kept
Thank you for allowing my lungs to continuously inhale and
exhale the gift of life
Thank you for never defining me by the world's standards
The way you see me is something the world could never
understand

A Dedication

To every hand that places this book in their palms and their eyes on my words, thank you. I know time is precious and too often we take it for granted. If you've reached this far, I've held an amount of yours. And because of that I am forever grateful.

To my Mom, favorite cousins and close friends. Your encouraging words have been pivotal throughout this book writing process. From the moment it was just an idea, to the manifestation of my creation today. You've been my biggest cheerleaders. I'm so thankful for your love and support.

Love,
Nia

This is the part where I tell you more about myself,

I'm a young woman trying to find my way through life. I have always enjoyed poetry. I lost touch with writing for years, until I ran into pain. I found a love for writing about my pain and making it rhyme. As time passed, I felt like it didn't matter if it rhymed. But more so how can I tell my raw truths. Truths that are hard to tell but seem easy to feel. I'm a pretty complex person to say the least. Most people know me as bubbly, energetic, and always hyper. Some have saw other sides of me which treaded alongside darkness. Despite the darkness, my goal was to push through and find the light. I feel that there's beauty in the journey of overcoming hard times to become better versions of ourselves. I hope you can take at least one thing away from my words I've tussled with late nights, early mornings and everything in between. Always remember no one can tell you how to do ART. And no one can tell you that your art is right or wrong.

Keep Up With My Social Networks

Instagram: @_iampurpose

Email: nia.crews@yahoo.com

Made in the USA
Middletown, DE
15 August 2019